VIOLA
101 DISNEY SONGS

Available for
FLUTE, CLARINET, ALTO SAX, TENOR SAX, TRUMPET,
HORN, TROMBONE, VIOLIN, VIOLA, CELLO

ISBN 978-1-5400-0241-9

The following songs are the property of:

Bourne Co.
Music Publishers
5 West 37th Street
New York, NY 10018

BABY MINE
GIVE A LITTLE WHISTLE
HEIGH-HO
HI-DIDDLE-DEE-DEE (AN ACTOR'S LIFE FOR ME)
I'M WISHING
I'VE GOT NO STRINGS
SOME DAY MY PRINCE WILL COME
WHEN I SEE AN ELEPHANT FLY
WHEN YOU WISH UPON A STAR
WHISTLE WHILE YOU WORK
WHO'S AFRAID OF THE BIG BAD WOLF?
WITH A SMILE AND A SONG

DISTRIBUTED BY

7777 W. BLUEMOUND RD. P.O. BOX 13819 MILWAUKEE, WI 53213

Visit Hal Leonard Online at
www.halleonard.com

CONTENTS

*Based on the "Winnie the Pooh" works,
by A. A. Milne and E. H. Shepard

**TARZAN® Owned by Edgar Rice Burroughs, Inc.
and Used by Permission.
© Burroughs/Disney

BABY MINE

from DUMBO

VIOLA

Words by NED WASHINGTON
Music by FRANK CHURCHILL

Moderately slow

THE BALLAD OF DAVY CROCKETT

from DAVY CROCKETT

Words by TOM BLACKBURN
Music by GEORGE BRUNS

Moderately

BELLA NOTTE
from LADY AND THE TRAMP

Music and Lyrics by PEGGY LEE
and SONNY BURKE

Slowly

BE OUR GUEST
from BEAUTY AND THE BEAST

VIOLA

Music by ALAN MENKEN
Lyrics by HOWARD ASHMAN

Moderately

BEAUTY AND THE BEAST

from BEAUTY AND THE BEAST

VIOLA

Music by ALAN MENKEN
Lyrics by HOWARD ASHMAN

Moderately slow

BELLE
from BEAUTY AND THE BEAST

VIOLA

Music by ALAN MENKEN
Lyrics by HOWARD ASHMAN

Moderately slow

BIBBIDI-BOBBIDI-BOO
(The Magic Song)
from CINDERELLA

Words by JERRY LIVINGSTON
Music by MACK DAVID and AL HOFFMAN

Brightly

BREAKING FREE
from HIGH SCHOOL MUSICAL

VIOLA

Words and Music by
JAMIE HOUSTON

BEST OF FRIENDS

from THE FOX AND THE HOUND

VIOLA

Words by STAN FIDEL
Music by RICHARD JOHNSTON

Moderately

CAN YOU FEEL THE LOVE TONIGHT

from THE LION KING

VIOLA

Music by ELTON JOHN
Lyrics by TIM RICE

Pop Ballad

CANDLE ON THE WATER

from PETE'S DRAGON

VIOLA

Words and Music by AL KASHA
and JOEL HIRSCHHORN

CHIM CHIM CHER-EE

from MARY POPPINS

VIOLA

Words and Music by RICHARD M. SHERMAN
and ROBERT B. SHERMAN

Lightly, with gusto

small notes optional

16

CIRCLE OF LIFE

from THE LION KING

VIOLA

Music by ELTON JOHN
Lyrics by TIM RICE

Moderately (with an African beat)

THE CLIMB
from HANNAH MONTANA: THE MOVIE

VIOLA

Words and Music by JESSI ALEXANDER
and JON MABE

Moderately slow

CRUELLA DE VIL
from 101 DALMATIANS

Words and Music by
MEL LEVEN

VIOLA

A DREAM IS A WISH YOUR HEART MAKES
from CINDERELLA

Words and Music by MACK DAVID,
AL HOFFMAN and JERRY LIVINGSTON

FEED THE BIRDS
(Tuppence a Bag)
from MARY POPPINS

Words and Music by RICHARD M. SHERMAN
and ROBERT B. SHERMAN

COLORS OF THE WIND
from POCAHONTAS

VIOLA

Music by ALAN MENKEN
Lyrics by STEPHEN SCHWARTZ

DO YOU WANT TO BUILD A SNOWMAN?

from FROZEN

VIOLA

Music and Lyrics by KRISTEN ANDERSON-LOPEZ
and ROBERT LOPEZ

DAYS IN THE SUN

from BEAUTY AND THE BEAST

VIOLA

Music by ALAN MENKEN
Lyrics by TIM RICE

small notes optional

Slower

EVERMORE
from BEAUTY AND THE BEAST

VIOLA

Music by ALAN MENKEN
Lyrics by TIM RICE

Moderately

HEIGH-HO
(The Dwarfs' Marching Song)
from SNOW WHITE AND THE SEVEN DWARFS

Words by LARRY MOREY
Music by FRANK CHURCHILL

Brightly, cheerfully

FOR THE FIRST TIME IN FOREVER

from FROZEN

VIOLA

Music and Lyrics by KRISTEN ANDERSON-LOPEZ
and ROBERT LOPEZ

Moderately, with excitement

Moderately, with expression

HI-DIDDLE-DEE-DEE
(An Actor's Life for Me)
from PINOCCHIO

Words by NED WASHINGTON
Music by LEIGH HARLINE

Brightly, in 2

FRIEND LIKE ME
from ALADDIN

VIOLA

Music by ALAN MENKEN
Lyrics by HOWARD ASHMAN

Bright Two-beat

GASTON
from BEAUTY AND THE BEAST

VIOLA

Music by ALAN MENKEN
Lyrics by HOWARD ASHMAN

Moderately slow, in 1

GOD HELP THE OUTCASTS

from THE HUNCHBACK OF NOTRE DAME

VIOLA

Music by ALAN MENKEN
Lyrics by STEPHEN SCHWARTZ

GIVE A LITTLE WHISTLE
from PINOCCHIO

Words by NED WASHINGTON
Music by LEIGH HARLINE

Moderately, in 2

GO THE DISTANCE

from HERCULES

VIOLA

Music by ALAN MENKEN
Lyrics by DAVID ZIPPEL

Slowly

HAKUNA MATATA

from THE LION KING

VIOLA

Music by ELTON JOHN
Lyrics by TIM RICE

HAPPY WORKING SONG
from ENCHANTED

VIOLA

Music by ALAN MENKEN
Lyrics by STEPHEN SCHWARTZ

D.C. al Coda

CODA

HE'S A PIRATE
from PIRATES OF THE CARIBBEAN: THE CURSE OF THE BLACK PEARL

VIOLA

Music by KLAUS BADELT,
GEOFFREY ZANELLI and HANS ZIMMER

HE'S A TRAMP
from LADY AND THE TRAMP

Words and Music by PEGGY LEE
and SONNY BURKE

Moderately

HOW DOES A MOMENT LAST FOREVER

from BEAUTY AND THE BEAST

VIOLA

Music by ALAN MENKEN
Lyrics by TIM RICE

Moderately

I JUST CAN'T WAIT TO BE KING

from THE LION KING

VIOLA

Music by ELTON JOHN
Lyrics by TIM RICE

Bright Two-beat

HOW FAR I'LL GO

from MOANA

VIOLA

Music and Lyrics by
LIN-MANUEL MIRANDA

Moderately, in 2

I'M LATE
from ALICE IN WONDERLAND

Words by BOB HILLIARD
Music by SAMMY FAIN

Moderately fast

I SEE THE LIGHT

from TANGLED

VIOLA

Music by ALAN MENKEN
Lyrics by GLENN SLATER

I'M WISHING
from SNOW WHITE AND THE SEVEN DWARFS

Words by LARRY MOREY
Music by FRANK CHURCHILL

Moderately slow, in 2

I'LL MAKE A MAN OUT OF YOU

from MULAN

VIOLA

Music by MATTHEW WILDER
Lyrics by DAVID ZIPPEL

Moderately

IN SUMMER
from FROZEN

VIOLA

Music and Lyrics by KRISTEN ANDERSON-LOPEZ
and ROBERT LOPEZ

Moderately, in 2

I'VE GOT A DREAM

from TANGLED

VIOLA

Music by ALAN MENKEN
Lyrics by GLENN SLATER

Moderately fast

IF I CAN'T LOVE HER

from BEAUTY AND THE BEAST: THE BROADWAY MUSICAL

VIOLA

Music by ALAN MENKEN
Lyrics by TIM RICE

IF I NEVER KNEW YOU
(End Title)
from POCAHONTAS

VIOLA

Music by ALAN MENKEN
Lyrics by STEPHEN SCHWARTZ

Moderately slow

I'VE GOT NO STRINGS
from PINOCCHIO

VIOLA

Words by NED WASHINGTON
Music by LEIGH HARLINE

IT'S A SMALL WORLD
from Disney Parks' "it's a small world" attraction

Words and Music by RICHARD M. SHERMAN
and ROBERT B. SHERMAN

KISS THE GIRL

from THE LITTLE MERMAID

VIOLA

Music by ALAN MENKEN
Lyrics by HOWARD ASHMAN

LAVA
from LAVA

VIOLA

Music and Lyrics by
JAMES FORD MURPHY

Moderately slow, in 2

LOVE IS AN OPEN DOOR
from FROZEN

VIOLA

Music and Lyrics by KRISTEN ANDERSON-LOPEZ
and ROBERT LOPEZ

LET IT GO
from FROZEN

VIOLA

Music and Lyrics by KRISTEN ANDERSON-LOPEZ
and ROBERT LOPEZ

Slowly, in 2

LAVENDER BLUE
(Dilly Dilly)
from SO DEAR TO MY HEART

VIOLA

Words by LARRY MOREY
Music by ELIOT DANIEL

MICKEY MOUSE MARCH
from THE MICKEY MOUSE CLUB

Words and Music by
JIMMIE DODD

LET'S GO FLY A KITE

from MARY POPPINS

Words and Music by RICHARD M. SHERMAN
and ROBERT B. SHERMAN

With gusto

THE LORD IS GOOD TO ME
from MELODY TIME

VIOLA

Words and Music by KIM GANNON
and WALTER KENT

Moderately

MY FUNNY FRIEND AND ME
from THE EMPEROR'S NEW GROOVE

Lyrics by STING
Music by STING and DAVID HARTLEY

Moderately

PART OF YOUR WORLD
from THE LITTLE MERMAID

VIOLA

Music by ALAN MENKEN
Lyrics by HOWARD ASHMAN

Moderately bright

66

MOTHER KNOWS BEST
from TANGLED

VIOLA

Music by ALAN MENKEN
Lyrics by GLENN SLATER

A PIRATE'S LIFE
from PETER PAN

Words by ED PENNER
Music by OLIVER WALLACE

RUMBLY IN MY TUMBLY

from THE MANY ADVENTURES OF WINNIE THE POOH

Words and Music by RICHARD M. SHERMAN
and ROBERT B. SHERMAN

Moderately bright

REFLECTION
from MULAN

VIOLA

Music by MATTHEW WILDER
Lyrics by DAVID ZIPPEL

THE SECOND STAR TO THE RIGHT

from PETER PAN

Words by SAMMY CAHN
Music by SAMMY FAIN

SEIZE THE DAY
from NEWSIES

VIOLA

Music by ALAN MENKEN
Lyrics by JACK FELDMAN

SO THIS IS LOVE
from CINDERELLA

VIOLA

Words and Music by AL HOFFMAN,
MACK DAVID and JERRY LIVINGSTON

Moderately

SO CLOSE
from ENCHANTED

VIOLA

Music by ALAN MENKEN
Lyrics by STEPHEN SCHWARTZ

Moderately slow, in 4

small note optional

Slowly, freely

THE SIAMESE CAT SONG

from LADY AND THE TRAMP

VIOLA

Words and Music by PEGGY LEE
and SONNY BURKE

Slowly

SOME DAY MY PRINCE WILL COME

from SNOW WHITE AND THE SEVEN DWARFS

Words by LARRY MOREY
Music by FRANK CHURCHILL

Moderately

SOMEDAY
from THE HUNCHBACK OF NOTRE DAME

VIOLA

Music by ALAN MENKEN
Lyrics by STEPHEN SCHWARTZ

SOMETHING THERE
from BEAUTY AND THE BEAST

VIOLA

Music by ALAN MENKEN
Lyrics by HOWARD ASHMAN

Moderately fast

A SPOONFUL OF SUGAR
from MARY POPPINS

VIOLA

Words and Music by RICHARD M. SHERMAN
and ROBERT B. SHERMAN

SUPERCALIFRAGILISTICEXPIALIDOCIOUS

from MARY POPPINS

VIOLA

Words and Music by RICHARD M. SHERMAN
and ROBERT B. SHERMAN

Brightly

"THIS IS ME."
from RATATOUILLE

VIOLA

Music by MICHAEL GIACCHINO

THAT'S HOW YOU KNOW
from ENCHANTED

VIOLA

Music by ALAN MENKEN
Lyrics by STEPHEN SCHWARTZ

TOYLAND MARCH
from BABES IN TOYLAND

Adapted from V. HERBERT Melody
Words by MEL LEVEN
Music by GEORGE BRUNS

March tempo

TRASHIN' THE CAMP
(Pop Version)
from TARZAN™

VIOLA

Words and Music by
PHIL COLLINS

THE UNBIRTHDAY SONG

from ALICE IN WONDERLAND

VIOLA

Words and Music by MACK DAVID,
AL HOFFMAN and JERRY LIVINGSTON

TRUE LOVE'S KISS
from ENCHANTED

VIOLA

Music by ALAN MENKEN
Lyrics by STEPHEN SCHWARTZ

Moderately

Bright Waltz

WESTWARD HO, THE WAGONS!

from WESTWARD HO, THE WAGONS!

Words by TOM BLACKBURN
Music by GEORGE BRUNS

WE BELONG TOGETHER
from TOY STORY 3

VIOLA

Music and Lyrics by
RANDY NEWMAN

WHEN I SEE AN ELEPHANT FLY
from DUMBO

Words by NED WASHINGTON
Music by OLIVER WALLACE

Moderately fast

D.S. al Fine
(take 2nd ending)

WE KNOW THE WAY

from MOANA

VIOLA

Music by OPETAIA FOA'I
Lyrics by OPETAIA FOA'I
and LIN-MANUEL MIRANDA

Moderately

A WHALE OF A TALE

from 20,000 LEAGUES UNDER THE SEA

VIOLA

Words and Music by NORMAN GIMBEL
and AL HOFFMAN

With a bounce

WE'RE ALL IN THIS TOGETHER

from HIGH SCHOOL MUSICAL

VIOLA

Words and Music by MATTHEW GERRARD
and ROBBIE NEVIL

WHISTLE WHILE YOU WORK
from SNOW WHITE AND THE SEVEN DWARFS

Words by LARRY MOREY
Music by FRANK CHURCHILL

Moderately bright

WHEN SHE LOVED ME
from TOY STORY 2

VIOLA

Music and Lyrics by
RANDY NEWMAN

Tenderly, very freely

WHEN YOU WISH UPON A STAR
from PINOCCHIO

VIOLA

Words by NED WASHINGTON
Music by LEIGH HARLINE

Moderately

WHEN WILL MY LIFE BEGIN?
from TANGLED

VIOLA

Music by ALAN MENKEN
Lyrics by GLENN SLATER

Moderately, in 2

Moderately slow (in 4)

Slowly, freely

WITH A SMILE AND A SONG
from SNOW WHITE AND THE SEVEN DWARFS

Words by LARRY MOREY
Music by FRANK CHURCHILL

Moderately slow, in 2

WHO'S AFRAID OF THE BIG BAD WOLF?

from THREE LITTLE PIGS

VIOLA

Words and Music by
FRANK CHURCHILL
Additional Lyric by ANN RONELL

Moderately, in 2

WINNIE THE POOH
from THE MANY ADVENTURES OF WINNIE THE POOH

Words and Music by RICHARD M. SHERMAN
and ROBERT B. SHERMAN

VIOLA

Tenderly

A WHOLE NEW WORLD

from ALADDIN

VIOLA

Music by ALAN MENKEN
Lyrics by TIM RICE

THE WONDERFUL THING ABOUT TIGGERS

VIOLA

from THE MANY ADVENTURES OF WINNIE THE POOH

Words and Music by RICHARD M. SHERMAN
and ROBERT B. SHERMAN

Very brightly

YO HO

(A Pirate's Life for Me)

from Disney Parks' Pirates of the Caribbean attraction

Words by XAVIER ATENCIO
Music by GEORGE BRUNS

In a robust manner

THEME FROM ZORRO
from the Television Series

Words by NORMAN FOSTER
Music by GEORGE BRUNS

Moderately, in 2

WRITTEN IN THE STARS
from AIDA

VIOLA

Music by ELTON JOHN
Lyrics by TIM RICE

YOU CAN FLY! YOU CAN FLY! YOU CAN FLY!

VIOLA

from PETER PAN

Words by SAMMY CAHN
Music by SAMMY FAIN

YOU ARE THE MUSIC IN ME

from HIGH SCHOOL MUSICAL 2

VIOLA

Words and Music by
JAMIE HOUSTON

Moderately fast Rock

YOU'LL BE IN MY HEART

(Pop Version)

from TARZAN™

VIOLA

Words and Music by
PHIL COLLINS

CODA

YOU'RE WELCOME

from MOANA

VIOLA

Music and Lyrics by
LIN-MANUEL MIRANDA

ZIP-A-DEE-DOO-DAH
from SONG OF THE SOUTH

Words by RAY GILBERT
Music by ALLIE WRUBEL

Brightly

ZERO TO HERO
from HERCULES

VIOLA

Music by ALAN MENKEN
Lyrics by DAVID ZIPPEL

YOU'VE GOT A FRIEND IN ME
from TOY STORY

VIOLA

Music and Lyrics by
RANDY NEWMAN

Easy Shuffle